DARKNESS INSIDE BRIGHTNESS

"EVERY JOURNEY OF LIFE IS A MYSTERIOUS NOVEL"

MUSKAN CHAUHAN

To all those who

dedicated me in the journey of words

and motivating me to pour my words in the

flowing journey of books............

Contents

Contents

Contents

Preface

"A journey of a beautiful string of words arranged in a thread making it shine in the darkness of the world where sorrows are kept hidden in the depth of wonders, a path full of struggles where we left our glory in the search of a knight with a motive behind to conquer the world of fairy tales where our souls stay hidden behind the story of music with that I hold to pen to write a world where our emotions travel in the depth of darkness.........."

Acknowledgements

" Acknowledging to all who have spread
love in my dark life,
making my life beautiful with a bed of roses"

Prologue

" A journey of flawless mountain caring great love in its warm embrace passing through a burrow of hurdles, where the mystery land stays in full of glory with the rainbow river"

1. Journey

" Journey, a path where we make life bright with full hurdles in the depth of puddles"

Journey to you

"Your every step made us surprised

Your every smile made us bright

Your every word, filled enthusiasm in us

Your every song, give a moral to us

Your every dance made us cheerful

Your every pain, made us cry

Your every care, melt our tension

Your every speech, made our sorrow disappear

Your every silence, made us tangle

Your every step, take us to heaven

Your every motivation filled us with joy

But when we decided to walk alone on a path

Your journey held a motivation for us"

Journey to know

"*You make the world know each other*

You make them stand for others

You always cared about them

Even though you are not there

But your words made them smile

You were the knight of their dark world

When you smiled at them through your pain

They twinkle like stars for you

When you got hurt

They feel your pain

When you work hard

They feel motivated to cherish the day

Your happiness

Made them make a key of confidence

And with ARMY held behind the reason to stay"

Journey of light

Struggle of life

Trembling of heart

Sorrow of fail

The journey of pain is yet to achieve

The days are passing

On a string of threads

Thoughts are kept

On a hanging wall

The meaning behind the tears

Is yet to achieve

The smile we kept

To hide our sorrow

In the depth of the burrow

The pride we kept

To achieve the spark

In the darkness of night

With the light of knight

Traveling on a path

To make a strike

We left the world

To make a claim"

2. Emotions

"Pain, sorrow, happiness are the key of the door where we have roller coaster full of struggles to deal with every key of emotion we take the journey to hurdles, to hide them we need to face the troubles"

Struggle for hurdles

"Journey travelled

With teary eyes

Struggling steps taken

With trembling heart

Journey on a cloud

In the world so wide

Dearly truth

Of darkness shadow

The fairy tale

Of utopian state

The pain of word

Is a densely sorrow

The holding hand

Are long forgotten

The journey of struggle

With an aim of hurdle"

Tears

"Journey of sorrow

In the books of sorrow

The diamond eyes

With glimmering tears

The blood-shedding

Through stabbed heart

The steps taken

To hold a knight

In the darkness of light

The cries of an owl

Heard in the dense forest

The pain it held

Is a mystery behind,

The group of herds

In the crowdie place

Was a tale

The journey of tears

Is still left behind"

3. Mystery of life

"The days passed, but the pain never fails
The sorrow I held scatters my heart
The pain I saw, are kept in my eyes
The losing fear, was my tale
Journey of happiness, is long forgotten
Days are passing, with no hope held behind
The mystery I solved are long forgotten
The Pandora box was opened
With no glory behind
Path travelled in the mist of darkness
Holding hands are lost in the crowd
But the truth of journey is kept mystery"

4. Fairy Tale

"We were a beautiful fairy tale
Blossoming flowers in a beautiful garden '
The shiny smile on a moon
Shimmering butterfly
Dancing buds on a plant
The story of someone's mystery
We were reborn to say the truth
The love we held was pride
The promises we made are kept together
But the secret of the journey is held behind"

5. Power of Promise

"The power of promise
The shine in the eyes
The glimmering tears
Pain of heart
Blood of love
Scattered sorrow
Was once my story
The gun I held
Was found a glory
But the sadness I hold
Is a mystery"

6. Broken Tale

"The pain of my heart
The blood flowed from the soul
Broken cries
With teary nights
The days I spend
Vanishing behind
The life I had
Is a story of broken pain
But the hope I gain
Still deep inside
The ignited light
Kept far away
My trembling legs
Making the path shaky
The trouble is my life
Making hurdles of bubble
The courage is kept
In the depth of the burrow
The pain I hide
Is a mystery story
The flow of blood
It making me weak

The day when it sparked

I lost my life

But the sorrow I held

Were swallowed by my darkness

The days I lost

Still mystery behind"

7. Stormy Night

"The stormy night
With glistening eyes
The shimmering stars
With galaxy in the eyes
The pearls left
Making a golden shade
The rainbow waterfall
Shows my identity
The harsh reality
Strike the society
With these strings of music
I left the journey
For a golden thread
Leaving society behind"

8. Beautiful Day

"The beautiful day
With blossoming stars
The beautiful day
With chirping melody
The beautiful day
With hurtful tears
The journey we took
Is left behind
The prideful words
Took a turn in my life
The hurtful words
Is challenging my heart"

9. Piercing Heart

"The piercing of a heavy stone
In my heart
The blood flowing through my veins
Is a heavy tear fall
The sharp pain in the soul
Is making me blind
With every step
My voice trembles
The call of an angel
Never reaches my ears
The days are passing
Are like a heavy burden
The darkness of the journey
Created a light
And with that, I snapped
With a final spark in my life
I left the brightness
for the darkness of life "

10. Darkness

"The darkness of night
Is indicating my pain
The twinkling of stars
Is showing my pain
The heat from the sun
Is showing my anger
The thunderstrike
Is showing my sorrowful voice
The drops of rain
Is showing my tears
But a beautiful day
Is showing happiness
With these emotions
I mend my heart
"

11. Love and Breaking

"Love in my heart
Is a painful sorrow
The day I claim myself as someone else
It felt like a nightmare to me
Flowing of tears held a strong meaning behind
Strength to unleash the pain
Darkness consuming me
Held the pride
The longing of the warmth
Making me tremble
The touch of fingers
Felt like a painful strike
The first words
Make my memory bittersweet
The flirty word
Make the memory bittersweet
Remembering your hurtful words
The day you left me
Hope inside was lost behind
Remembering the nights
I cried my pain
The painful cries I held in my heart

Making the soul ache

But the words left behind my mind

Were all lies

The journey we took together

I left behind

With these thoughts

I took a new step in my life"

12. Sweet Bitter Pain

"The darkness of life
The shimmering of teary eyes
The trembling soul
Heartfelt moments
With a prideful smile
The lost journey
In the dense forest
The darkest pain
Stabbing deep in the heart
My love for art
Is left behind
The faith inside
Is yet to destroy
But the journey of a knight
Is hurtful pride
The moments of sorrow
Are passed behind
The journey of emotions
It making me cry
The bunch full words
Are stabbed behind
The days are passing

In the journey of truth

With that, I lost my soul behind

”

13. Flowing Emotions

"The water flowing through my eye
Seems like a flowing river
The darkness of the soul
Seem like a night
The stabbing pain
Feels deeper in the heart
The journey of true emotions
Is full of struggles
The pain in mind
Is sweet bitter
The stinging pain in the eyes
Reminds me of my past
But every dark angel
Are like my friends
Welcoming me into a beautiful world"

14. Sadness Consumed

"The passing hours
Feels like a sorrowful journey
The pain in my heart
Feels bitter
The truthful journey
Feels dividing pain
The sorrowful moment
Stabbing of hearts
Cries of soul
With the pain of darkness
Is consuming my mind
The bitter moment of life
Is hurtful pride
I am traveling on a long path
With latten in soul
Finding a knight
In a dense forest
The journey I took
Is full of the thorny path
But the fire in my heart
Is full of emotions"

15. Sorrow in heart

"Flowing tears from my eyes
Is a painful sorrow
the journey of a river
is flawless pain
Stabbing pain in my heart
is the hardest reality
the discoveries of doors
with trembling hands
The fighting sorrows
with harsh words
making me shiver in the cold
the beauty behind the mask
is the journey of emotions
the fight among the knights
is a blood bath
with beautiful flower
comes striking terror
making heart melt
in the depth of sorrow"

16. Far Destiny

"Traveling on a path
cherry blossom in the desert
destiny near me
but still so far
teary eyes
blurry views
trembling heart
with a beautiful path
Traveling mountains
with shaky steps
destiny is still so far
burrow made
with a depth of hate
sparky eyes
vanishing pain
in this dense dessert
forest made by the bloody path
is a hiding place of darkness
vampire soul
in this fairy tale
destiny is still so far"

17. Faith in Believe

"Faith and believe
are the keywords of sorrow
Pain and wound
are left behind
The journey which was started
come at halt
The people once I loved
leaving me behind
making me broken
but still, I mend myself
and left for the journey "

18. Truth of Life

"Emptiness is converted into darkness
life is traveling in the hole
the journey is long
struggles are at every step
but the strength
dedication towards the aim
making me tangle"

"Traveling at a distance
voyaging to a mystery
diving in love
hiding the pain of sorrow
making an introvert heart
forgiving the past
that's the life I live long"

19. Burrow in Sorrow

"The day without a sorrow
in the depth of burrow
the day with pain
in the wide plain
making me insane
I am trying so hard
to win the card
but the destiny is keeping far
to reach the bar
of hope
in the world full of rope
I wanted to cry
but wanted to make a fly
In this densely desert
walking like a lost soul
making a foul
but at last, I reach the aim
and make a claim "

20. World of Emotions

"The world is sparkling
the stars are twinkling
The flower is blooming
with your smile
your every step
making us breathe
in the deep
we remember your pledge
the days are passing
the nights are calling
but the duty we have
is stoping us to take a step"

21. Hope in Cloud

"Walking on a cloud
with a voice so loud
holding a hand
but fall on the land
it made me cry
but wanted to fly
wished to go back
with the strength, I lack
to get the pack
but it made the world spark
and get the world dark
wanted a light
but forgot the height
to go back to my knight
with the falling of night
wanted a hope
getting a nope
so, I decided to wait
but it is getting so late
with that, I left the place
to get a pace
and decided to make an aim

to get it to claim"

22. Trouble

"Life is making a trouble
in this world of hurdle
to get out of the puddle
to break the bubble
I am trying so hard
to get a start
it is my last
to breathe so fast
worrying so wide
in the world to hide
it is making me shy
I left to cry
but decided to fly
waiting for the spark
in this world so dark
wanting to hold a hand
to make a land
but getting the silence
to break the violence
in the world of war
making me nervous
to make the balance

in this life

getting a sharpening

so, I left to find my knight

in the darkness of night

and with that, I made a flight

to find my aim

and to make a claim ”

23. Never belong to you

"The teary eyes, never belong to you
The sad smile, never belong to you
The dull day, never belong to you
The dried roses, never belong to you
The shining stars, never belong to you
But the day you achieve them
You never belong to the world"

24. Miss You Alot

"We met on the path
Where I need a light
I found you
When I was falling apart
You gave strength
In my dark
We made many promises
But never made them true
And suddenly you left me alone
On the path of thrones
I told you about my sorrows
And you always stood there for me
But at the ending of the day
I found I lost you in this dense world"

•

25. Angel's Love

"The tears shedding from an eye
The voice muffled by a pillow
The cry of an angel
For a devil to return
For the love of her life
The truth kept untold
Are yet to be opened
The days are passing
Souls of the kingdom have loosed their hope
Yet a person is standing at a window
Shouting for her love
The cries left from her mouth
Doesn't reach her lover but t reach the sky
They are shedding the tears of pain
In the separation of two love souls
Then there came a spark
Making the flower blossom
That spread a smile on everyone's face
Because it was the light of devil's power
That was the time when the god was forced to send a soul back
The love of a life

The pain of a knife

Shouting for the knight

In the darkness of the night

It was the time when the two souls unite"

26. Go Away

"Showering with tears
Dancing in drops
Laughing with a cry
All I hear is pain and pain
Borrowing a shelter
Crying with throat dry
All I want is the to pain go away"

27. Lost Life

"The loneness of life
Is sharpening of a knife
In the search of the knight
I lost my nights
I held my cry
To make a fly
But I lost the key
To make me free"

28. Pain

"The day is shinning
The night is twinkling
But my eyes are tearing
The flowers are blossoming
Nature is blooming
But my life is struggling
The days are passing by
To make me cry
I want to fly
But I got a pry
I lost my soul
In the game of goal
By the time I reach the pole
In the search of the role
I lost my life
In the shoot of knife
I went to search knight
In the darkness of night"

29. The day you

"The day you call me
I came to you
The day you send me a message
I received it
The day you missed me
I respond you
The day you spend with me
I miss them
The day you stand with me
I show respect to you
The day you smile
I embrace it with me
The day you left me
I feel my heart shattered"

30. I Remember you

"I remember your every smile
Like you were still there with me now
I remember your every word
Like you are there with me
I remember the moment we spent together
Like you are holding me
I remember the painful thoughts you shared with me
Like you wanted to pour out your soul to me
I remember your sorrow
Like want you wanted to share your darkness with me
I remember your every teary eye
Like you want to shed but don't got the chance
I remember your every care
You gave to me
I remember your every hug
Like you wanted to share something with me
I remember every happiness that you spend with me
That made me teary
I remember you and always being there with you
To hold you tight and say
'I love you buddy'"

31. Are Still

"The memories I spend with you
Are you still with me
The tears I hold for you
Are still there
The smile I kept for you
Are still present
The shinning eyes which I show you
Are still there
The pains I hide in my heart
Are still there in my heart
The pains I hide to make you smile
Are you still in mind
The thoughts of holding your hands
Are still in my remembrance
The promises we made with each other
Are still kept with me
The diaries I wrote with you
Are you still with me
But the day you left me, the sorrow of life
Are you still with me
And with that, I continue my journey"

32. True Me

"The smile on my face
Is hiding the tears
The shine in my eyes
Are hiding the tiredness
But when the makeup got remove
I cried my whole heart out"

33. Memory Still Hold

"Holding a hand
And walking in a park
We sat under a tree
I said I love you-
Before I complete my words
You left my hand
And walked away from me
I tried to reach you
But you faded away
I was crying to reach you
But you said you will come again
So, I sat there you and waited for you
But you near came
On that day I realize that I lost you
But I prayed to God that I want you back
And said
I love you Grandma "

34. Still With Memory of Grandma

"The day I lost you
I realized the world is becoming dark for me
The day I wanted to say 'I love you
I was forced to say I lost you
The day I wanted to enjoy with you
I was crying in the corner
The day you make me realize you were there for me
I was trying to hold your hand
But the next day I came to realize
That you left me in the pool of darkness."

35. Life

““My life novel is carrying many sorrowful moments but the truth of reality is making it difficult to understand””

““The book I once read has lost its beauty, but the novel I am writing held the darkness””

““Many people come and go but the pain they left never fades away””

““My life is full of happiness but the day I realize it was a dream it breaks me apart””

““My heart is breaking day by day because the pain I am carrying is swelling it to burst””

““My mind is making me crazy but my heart is holding me tight””

““I cry at night and smile at the light but when the evening comes I see people laughing at me””

36. Fighting and Struggling

"Life makes us sad
And that is so bad
We are taking the pain
To hold the gain
Life is pushing us back
But we hold our pack
We hold our cry
To make a fly
Once we found our aim
We take the claim
With that, we found our path
And left for bath"

37. World Left Behind

"The day is coming soon
Making the life full moon
Helping us to bloom
To make our life gloom
In the night
Our light is bright
Waiting for our departure
To make our future
Helping hands fade away
But we will find them back one day
The people we know are making us sad
By leaving our hand
We try to hold them
But the school end
Our journey start
With a new step
Leaving them behind
In the glory of a mysterious journey"

38. Beauty of World

"The world is twinkling like a star
And brightening like a sun
Blossoming like flowers
Chirping like birds
And
Coming together like drops falling in the river
To meet its siblings
But we all know there is always
A reason behind everything
And have a meaning behind the reason
Every meaning have words of nature
But the words can only be imagined
The real enjoyment of every word of nature
Comes from heart"

39. Hold you Tight

"When the world ask me to leave you
I hold the thread tight
When the world went against me
I found your motivation with me
When the world ignores me
I got your supportive words standing along with me
When others gave me disappointment
I found a reason to sat from you
When they put me down
You were there to hold me
When I found myself depress
You make me cherish that moment with bright light
When I lost my way to reach
That day I lost my breath"

40. Lost in World of Death

"When someone scolds me
I become sad
I feel thinking bad
I feel like hell
I feel depressed
I try to take my breath
But think about my dad
If I die he feels be sad
So, I try to stay
But the day my inner soul burst
My thoughts come first
I live in the dark
But one day there came a spark
My life becomes bright
In the darkness of light
A torch held in the shadow
In the depth of the burrow
I see myself under the bark
And with the last string of sorrow
I left the world in the depth of burrow"

41. World of Sadness

"Life is making us sad,
And that's so bad
We are taking the pain,
To hold the gain
Life is pushing us back,
And it's so bad
But we hold our pack
We are taking the pain
To hold the gain
Life is cherishing us
In the full of bus
We hold our cry
To make a fly
Once we found our aim
We made a claim
We found the left the path,
and left for the task"

42. They Do Care

"I was sitting near a beach, imagining my dreams.
I was closing my eyes, holding my memories tight.
The deep I was going, the more I was leaving the world behind.
I was relaxing my mind, to hold them tight.
Until I realize someone holding me tight, I shoot open my eyes.
Dangling my hands wide, stood with my shaky legs.
But the person who was standing in front of me
Made quite nervous of my act
I left out a shaky chuckle, but they give me reassuring smile
Making my nerves calm, in the densely forest
Without any words, I throw myself in their arms
While saying them 'I hate them', for leaving me behind
But they hold me tight, saying that they love me
Making my tear vanish with their slight touch
And fluttering my heart with their love
But all did I was crying in their arms
Until I realize that it was just a dream
And they left me alone in this wide world…."

43. Nature in Quotes

"There will be a stormy night in our life when the path will be washed away but we will have a hope of bright light in our dark world so keep smiling and facing the hurdles......"

"The twinkling stars remind me of my bright days but an empty sky reminds me of my hurdles at that moment I pick up my brush and paint my beautiful world where there are no sorrows....."

"Every step of failure takes you to the world of success..."

"Every single hour can teach you a new lesson......."

"don't shed the tears for your failed step, store them for your success..."

"The sky is turning dark and the time is passing so slow which is making me feel terrible and annoyed as I want it to be passed as soon as possible....."

"The days are passing making me tired but the new light of every day is looking special to me which forced me to think that everything is good......"

44. Prophecy Story

"prophecy was true
it was indeed true
a true reality for an unborn girl
who never came into the world when the prophecy was made
it was like the sky was telling a story
it was a story
for a girl and her family
it was telling the future of a couple
telling the pain of a mother
telling a soft lullaby for deep slumber
but time travels too fast
the time came soon and no one was able to stop the words
left from an angel's mouth
a demon disguise
a father of the new ruler
Who never wants his child to love anyone
who wants his child to live a lonely life
a man who killed his wife
as she was the only weapon to kill the cruel demon
she was born to kill the demon angel
but soon she fell in love with the enemy

she was left behind from the reality

she never came to knew that she was the chosen girl

but reality hits hard when all the life you were kept in the dark

from the person, we love with our whole heart

we are left behind with a broken heart

when destiny played its role when the truth strikes at your door,

when you came to know

that the person you love never loved you

but you need to be strong for your born child the true heir of the kingdom

you are left behind with the pledge to make your child a king

who will take the pledge

to save its the kingdom from every evil

who will always stand for justice

and she did that

but destiny never allowed her to watch her son become a strong king

although he has a cold heart he never let any of his subjects feel sorrow

he was always ready to sacrifice his life for

he truly worshipped by the kingdom

the journey was starting shows its beautiful nature soon the kingdom found its the queen

and here the journey began............ ”

45. Fairy Tale of Sadness

"Life is a full of a mysterious journey
we are not aware of what the future holds for us,
it superstitious mist of densely mind,
the strong hurdle steps,
the trembling voice and the pain in the bleeding heart,
the painful cry of the barren mother is piercing through the soul of heaven.
The cries of a mother who is stabbed in front of her innocent,
the last goodbye of painful cries,
the shaky hands swiping the beads of golden tears and
with the last suck of breath soul left the angelic body,
once a beautiful face of women,
a mother of her brave
innocent child is now left behind with a painful smile,
the last breath
the body that runs behind
the child with fitful of giggles is thrown
on the dirt like a light cloth blown in the air with a heavy storm.
The child who was left behind
the world full of thorns is now a king of the world,

ruling the kingdom which once was a dream of her late mother.
A boy,
once who was cheerful soul is turned into a cold wall of barrier,
the fitful giggles are now replaced by the harsh tone
but the thing which never changed is the beautiful heart
the strong determination to rule the kingdom
with great honesty making the subjects to held pride in him.
Sadly everything vanished once again like thin air,
a beautiful love came into his life
but everything turned into ashes after the prophecy was assigned,
once again the past was repeated itself,
the dense sorrow of a mother losing her life in front of her beautiful innocent
the person whom he loves with her dearly heart is once again left.
The life was taken the husband lose his mind,
making him emotionless.
On that day he took a pledge to destroy the world for his dear wife
the child who lost her mother.
The history was repeated so was the pain
his life was increased
once he lost his mother and now a beautiful wife."

46. True Color

"“Every corner of world filled with sorrow yet the meaning behind them is deeply buried, the hope of finding the true color

life is a journey of sorrowful and bright moments.

The day without pain is like a journey without morals,

the thorny paths are painful journeys but the result behind it is a soul full of the journey with a beautiful shimmering.”"

47. Motivation

"whenever we get lost
you motivated us
whenever we feel pain
you cherished us
whenever we went or feel alone
you hold us
whenever we fall down
you were there for us
whenever we went wrong
you made us right
we all know you are with us
and we purple....."

48. Darkness of Life

"*The darkness of night*
Is indicating my pain
The twinkling of stars
Is showing my pain
The heat from the sun
Is showing my anger
The thunderstrike
Is showing my sorrowful voice
The drops of rain
Is showing my tears
But a beautiful day
Is showing happiness
With these emotions
I mend my heart
"

49. Journey to Shine

"Paradise in heaven
Justice in sea
The position we held,
is yet to achieve.
The days are passing
Night is screaming
the pain of the journey,
is making us tremble.
yet the position in heaven,
is to achieve.
The struggling of paths,
are passing with trembling hearts.
The darkest hour,
is giving us hope of the brightest star.
The journey of word
making us proud
The wild crowd,
is scaring us to depth.
But with a trembling voice
we determined our steps
and with that, we left for our aim
to make a claim

in the world so wide

with the darkness of mind

exploring the night

with a sharp knife

and the depth of knight

we held our journey

to claim a fight

”

50. Cries of an owl

"Every night an owl cries a story of pain
telling the journey of sorrow
in the world of the burrow
where life is so dark
traveling on a path
is so hard
getting motivation
in the depth of hurdles
on the bubble of a puddle
making a heart tremble
with blurry eyes
continued the journey
in a hurry
to find a light
in the darkness of night
but still, hear the sound
cries of an owl"

Printed by Libri Plureos GmbH in Hamburg, Germany